Publisher's Preface

Robert Gallagher
Publisher
Saint Benedict Press, LLC
TAN Books

With this booklet on hand as an introduction, we pray you will be able to develop an authentic Marian spirituality. From the Cross, Jesus gave us Mary to be our spiritual Mother, and He wishes us to develop a deep appreciation and love for her. He is calling us through the writings of St. Louis de Montfort to an intimate and profound relationship with Himself through a "true devotion" to Mary, our Blessed Mother.

The Classics Made Simple series aims to introduce the great works of Catholic literature to a wide readership. The Classics of the Faith are not meant only for saints and scholars: they're meant for everyone. They're wise, human, practical, and they have something important to say to each of us.

The Classics are also timeless. Other books come and go, passing with the tastes and fads of each generation. But the Catholic Classics remain and God has used them to teach and sanctify men and women of every age.

We hope this *TAN Guide* will stir within you a desire to read *True Devotion to Mary*, or if you've already read it, to re-read it with a renewed interest. You'll discover each *TAN Guide* is a perfect vehicle to introduce your newest favorite Classic to your friends and family. Give this little booklet a few minutes of your time and see what happens!

"To go to Jesus through Mary is truly to honor Jesus Christ. It indicates that we do not esteem ourselves worthy of approaching His infinite holiness directly, that we need Mary to be our Mediatrix with Him, our Mediator."

—St. Louis de Montfort

Introduction to—*True Devotion to Mary*

What image does the word "devotion" conjure up in our minds? Isn't it often a tepid one, a vague idea of emotional religiosity? Isn't our image of a devout person something like this: a little old lady who scrupulously says her Rosary and other prayers every day, haunts her church premises, lights candles, smiles sweetly, and oozes sentimentality? We might admire such devout souls, even as we reflect uneasily that if this is devotion we must not be cut out for it.

Real devotion, however—the "true devotion" preached by St. Louis de Montfort—is a very different thing. There is nothing sentimental about it, because it is primarily an *orientation of the mind and the will*, and need not involve emotions at all. As Catholics, we know that love of God is the "first and greatest commandment," as Jesus said. This starts with keeping the commandments of God and of the Church, of course, but how does one acquire *devotion*: the gift of divine love that makes the practice of our religion the principle means of an ever closer union with God, one that transforms all of life? We sometimes think that such love is only for the saints, and not for the likes of us. On the contrary, St. Louis de Montfort teaches, devotion is for every single one of us.

To Jesus, Through Mary

All right, we should begin to love God more than we have in the past; how shall we do it, though? St. Louis first points the way in one of his lesser-known works, *The Love of Eternal Wisdom*. In that book, he discusses four means of achieving a true Christian life in this world, the last of which leads to the subject matter of *True Devotion to Mary*. "The greatest means of all," he writes, "and the most wonderful of all secrets for obtaining and keeping Divine Wisdom, is a tender and true devotion to the Blessed Mary." He goes so far as to say that "through Mary alone, then, can we obtain possession of Wisdom." She is the necessary mediator between us, sinful souls groping towards the Divine Light, her Son.

St. Louis goes on to say that he has never found a devotional practice more solid than this one, because it is based on the example of Christ Himself, who loved His mother so much. In *True Devotion to Mary*, he sums up the essence of his teaching on Our Lady: "The more a soul is consecrated to Mary, the more it will be consecrated to Jesus Christ. It is for this reason that the perfect consecration to Jesus Christ is nothing else than a perfect and entire consecration of oneself to the Most Blessed Virgin, which is the devotion I teach." This, then, is the theme of *True Devotion*, developed by a master of the spiritual life. St. Louis explains why Marian devotion is necessary for us, the distinction between true and false devotion, how we go about acquiring the real thing, and what results we can expect.

A Classic from the Age of Mary

The published work, *True Devotion to Mary*, has an intriguing history. The original manuscript was lost after St. Louis's death in 1716, and recovered by chance in 1842, by one of the priests of the congregation founded by the Saint. Interestingly, St. Louis seems to have foreseen that something like that would happen, because Satan hated and feared the little work. "I clearly foresee," wrote St. Louis, "that raging brutes will come in fury to tear with their diabolical teeth this little writing and him whom the Holy Ghost has made use of to write it, or at least, to envelop it in the silence of a coffer in order that it may not appear." He also foretold, however, that someday it would reappear and be widely read.

The fact that it reappeared in the mid-nineteenth century places it within the extraordinary "Age of Mary," which spanned the hundred-year period from the early nineteenth to the early twentieth century and was characterized by numerous approved apparitions of Our Lady. Starting with the Miraculous Medal apparitions on the Rue du Bac in Paris in 1830, the Virgin Mary's appearances continued at La Salette in 1846, Lourdes in 1858, Pontmain in 1871, and

The World Prepares for the Age of Mary

1673
Louis born in Brittany (France).

1678
Dutch mathematician, astronomer, and physicist Christiaan Huygens publishes his *Treatise on Light*, introducing his argument that light consists of waves.

1676-1689
The pontificate of Innocent XI reforms Vatican administration by reducing expenses, eliminating nepotism, and streamlining decision-making.

1685
Three great composers born: Johann Sebastian Bach, Georg Friederich Handel, and Domenico Scarlatti; their cantatas, operas, sonatas, and more will grace the next several decades.

Fatima in 1917. (There were still other authentic apparitions, but these are the main ones.) The Age of Mary also saw the official definition of some of the great doctrines of our Faith related to Mary, including her Immaculate Conception in 1854 and her Assumption in 1950.

It is clear that God in modern times has been repeatedly—almost urgently—calling attention to His Blessed Mother, to her role as our intercessor, and to His desire that we practice devotion to her. Of course, there are many ways of practicing Marian devotion, including the Rosary, Mass, meditation on the First Saturdays, and many other traditional practices. At the heart of these good practices, however, must be a truly fervent love for our heavenly mother that can transform our lives and keep us always faithful. St. Louis writes, in fact, that "devotion to our Blessed Lady is necessary for salvation and that it is an infallible mark of reprobation to have no esteem and love for the holy Virgin."

Thus he wrote his little book in order to lead souls to the kind of devotion that can most help them please God and save their souls. No wonder the Devil hated it! All the more reason why we should study *True Devotion to Mary* and put it into practice.

Devotion is Necessary for Salvation
The several brief introductions to the work should be read before beginning the treatise itself, particularly the one by the translator, Father Frederick Faber. Father Faber was himself a great writer, and the author of several classics of spirituality that have appealed to generations of readers.

1685
Louis sent to study at Jesuit college in Rennes.

1700
Louis ordained a priest at the age of twenty-seven; begins ministry as hospital chaplain.

1700
Louis joins the Third Order of the Dominicans.

1691-1694

Andrea Pozzo paints the illusionist ceiling fresco known as *Allegory of the Missionary Work of the Jesuits* in the Church of Sant'Ignazio in Rome, marking the culmination of the High Baroque artistic movement.

1701

Joseph Sauveur, French mathematician and physicist, presents the results of his research in acoustics, measuring and explaining the vibrations of musical tones.

Each chapter of the book is divided into short sub-chapters, making it easy to focus on the points the author is making. St. Louis's task in his introduction and in the first part of the work is to explain to readers Mary's greatness, and how necessary she is in the plan of salvation. God designed His plan this way, choosing Mary to bring His Son into the world and to be His instrument in sanctifying souls. She is therefore most necessary to us, as St. Louis concludes on the authority of the Fathers, Doctors, and saints of the Church: she is "necessary to all men to attain salvation."

To someone who has not previously been exposed to these ideas, they may come as a disconcerting surprise, and even arouse skepticism. In fact, we're not used to hearing nowadays the doctrine that St. Louis presents, although it rests on unimpeachable authority and on the age-old Tradition of the Church. As readers, we should be patient. The author explains exactly what he means when he states that devotion to Mary is absolutely necessary for us, whether we are saints or ordinary people and, in chapter two, outlines various aspects of the devotion. He makes a key point in the beginning of that chapter that it is important to note: the purpose and end of our devotion to Mary is not to make of her a sort of god, a rival to Jesus, but to bring us closer to Jesus, to whom all our devotions are ordered. He is our final end, but the most powerful and efficacious means for getting there is by devotion to His Mother.

The subsequent chapters describe various features of this devotion and the motives that might prompt us to practice

The World Prepares for the Age of Mary

1703

Antonio Vivaldi becomes violin master at Venice's Pio Ospedale della Pietà (La Pieta) orphanage, and writes over 400 concertos in four decades there.

1705
Louis commences seventeen years of traveling and preaching missions.

ARTICLES
OF
UNION,

1707

The Treaty of Union politically joins England, Scotland, and Wales in the United Kingdom of Great Britain.

1709

The great Italian harpsichord maker Bartolomeo Cristofori invents the pianoforte, precursor to the modern piano.

it as our way to Christ and to Heaven. Like St. Thérèse of Lisiuex and her "Little Way," St. Louis reminds us that true devotion "is a short way"—a spiritual short-cut, as it were, as compared with other more difficult and complicated forms of spirituality. It is heartening to read in later chapters of the marvelous effects true devotion will have on our lives, and the variety of practices we might adopt. The last section of the book is devoted to preparation for making a Total Consecration to Mary. In addition to the author's suggestions and practical advice, he includes several relevant passages from the Gospels and *The Imitation of Christ*, along with various prayers and litanies, and finally the Consecration prayer itself.

Devotion Versus the Reformation

Frequently St. Louis's focus is to move the reader to a tender love for Our Lady, upon which he lays great stress. This may surprise some modern readers who have grown up with the idea of Mary as our merciful mother who is always willing to hear our prayers. We're so used to thinking of her with affection that we don't understand why St. Louis keeps emphasizing the point.

Here we need to keep in mind the religious atmosphere in which he was writing. Since the Protestant Reformation of the previous century, the sixteenth, criticism of everything Catholic was promulgated by both preachers of the various non-Catholic sects and by the press. In France, Calvinism—with its stern theology and dislike of Catholic "pomp" and "superstitious devotions"—had long been disparaging love of the saints and, particularly, of Our Lady. Calvinist ideas

1713

Pope Clement XI publishes the papal bull *Unigentius Dei Filius*, condemning Jansenism and excommunicating many of its followers. Jansenism emphasized predestination, denied free will, and maintained that human nature is incapable of good.

1714

Gabriel Fahrenheit invents the mercury thermometer, greatly increasing the range and accuracy of temperature measurement. Later he will invent the temperature scale that bears his name.

1716
Louis dies at Saint Laurent sur Sevre.

1715
Louis founds the Sisters of Wisdom and the Company of Mary.

had even seeped into the Church in the form of Jansenism, which echoed some of the puritanical notions of the Calvinists. Since St. Louis knew that many of his readers might be influenced, even unconsciously, by such disparagement of tender love for Our Lady, he goes to some lengths to portray her as truly our mother, willing to listen to us, and always solicitous for our well-being.

The historical context in which he was writing might also explain St. Louis's concern to root devotion in Scripture, which Protestants accused Catholics of ignoring or not understanding, and likewise his precise descriptions of Church teachings about Mary. It was most important for his readers to understand the importance of the Bible in Catholic thought and practice, including such practices as praying to Our Lady and the saints, in

The World Prepares for the Age of Mary

1719

Daniel Defoe publishes his adventure novel *Robinson Crusoe*, which marks the beginning of realistic fiction as a literary genre.

1742

Edmond Hoyle's *Short Treatise on the Game of Whist* becomes the definitive text on the popular card game, a precursor to bridge.

1947
St. Louis de Montfort canonized by Pope Pius XII.

1904

Pope Piux X issues the key Marian encyclical *Ad Diem Illum* in commemoration of the fiftieth anniversary of the dogma of the Immaculate Conception; it relies heavily on the views expressed in de Montfort's book *True Devotion to Mary*.

order to be able to answer Protestant or Jansenist criticisms.

It was also essential for St. Louis's readers to realize that devotion to Mary could not be separated from the worship and love of Jesus Christ. The notion that Catholics made of Mary a sort of goddess whom they worshipped in the place of God was (and remains) a common Protestant calumny against the Church. In promoting devotion to Mary, St. Louis was also providing a defense of Catholic teaching on many points. Thus, reading *True Devotion* is an educational experience as well as an exercise of piety. We don't know whether any Calvinists or Jansenists bothered to read it, but if they had, it would have corrected many of their false notions about both the Catholic Faith and popular spirituality.

Certainly the many saints of the seventeenth century, a period so rich in sanctity, were all devoted to the Mother of God and promoted devotion to her in their various ways. It was an age in which Our Lord seemed anxious to promote recourse to His mother, perhaps with a view to arming the faithful against the cold and violent age that was about to dawn. Practicing the *True Devotion* of St. Louis became one of the most popular means of spiritual warfare in that age, and remains so unto our own. ◆

DID YOU KNOW?

True Devotion to Mary
*has been translated into over
thirty languages.*

Prayer to St. Louis De Montfort

Great Apostle and Lover of our Blessed Lady, St. Louis De Montfort, whose one desire was to set the world aflame with love for Jesus through Mary, we entreat you to obtain for us childlike, persevering, perfect devotion to Mary, so as to share in Mary's faith, hope, and charity, and to receive the favor we beseech you to obtain for us.

Love Mary, Glorify God

An excerpt from *True Devotion to Mary*

By this practice, faithfully observed, you will give Jesus more glory in a month than by any other practice, however difficult, in many years; and I give the following reasons for it:

1. Because, doing your actions by our Blessed Lady, as this practice teaches you, you abandon your own intentions and operations, although good and known, to lose yourself, so to speak, in the intentions of the Blessed Virgin, although they are unknown. Thus you enter by participation into the sublimity of her intentions, which are so pure that she gives more glory to God by the least of her actions—for example, in twirling her distaff or pointing her needle—than St. Lawrence by his cruel martyrdom on the gridiron, or even all the saints by all their heroic actions put together. It was thus that, during her sojourn here below, she acquired such an unspeakable aggregate of graces and merits that it were easier to count the stars of the firmament, the drops of water in the sea or the grains of sand upon its shore, than her merits and graces. Thus it was that she gave more glory to God than all the angels and saints have given Him or ever will give Him. O prodigy of a Mary! Thou canst not help but do prodigies of grace in souls that wish to lose themselves altogether in thee!

2. Because the soul in this practice counts as nothing whatever it thinks or does of itself, and puts its trust and takes its pleasures only in the dispositions of Mary, when it approaches Jesus or even speaks to Him. Thus it practices humility far more than the souls who act of themselves and trust, with however imperceptible a complacency, in their own dispositions. But if the soul acts more humbly, it there-

fore more highly glorifies God, who is perfectly glorified only by the humble and those that are little and lowly in heart.

3. Because our Blessed Lady, being pleased, out of great charity, to receive the present of our actions in her virginal hands, gives them an admirable beauty and splendor. Moreover, she offers them herself to Jesus Christ, and it is evident that Our Lord is thus more glorified by them than if we offered them by our own criminal hands.

4. Lastly, because you never think of Mary without Mary's thinking of God for you. You never praise or honor Mary without Mary's praising and honoring God with you. Mary is altogether relative to God; and indeed, I might well call her the relation to God. She only exists with reference to God. She is the echo of God that says nothing, repeats nothing, but God. If you say "Mary," she says "God." St. Elizabeth praised Mary, and called her blessed, because she had believed. Mary, the faithful echo of God, at once intoned: "My soul doth magnify the Lord" (Luke 1:46).

That which Mary did then, she does daily now. When we praise her, love her, honor her or give anything to her, it is God who is praised, God who is loved, God who is glorified, and it is to God that we give, through Mary and in Mary. ◆

The Life of St. Louis de Montfort

Louis-Marie Grignion de Montfort was born in 1673 and died in 1716. He survived a number of attempts on his life while writing his most enduring work, just as the book survived after the manuscript was initially lost.

From his childhood, spent in the northwest French region of Bretagne, Louis was always attracted to good works: particularly relief of the poor, who had a particularly difficult time making ends meet in that tumultuous time during the Wars of Religion following the Protestant Reformation. At twenty-seven, Louis was ordained a priest and became a hospital chaplain. The hospital was run wretchedly, and Father Louis found himself organizing the patients, first for purely devotional activities and then later as a sort of administrator.

In 1705, the young priest discovered his true calling, which was preaching—to people of all classes, all over western France. For the last eleven years of his life, "the father with the big Rosary" and the pilgrim staff adorned with an image of Mary was constantly on the move, preaching and giving missions in villages, towns, and cities, wherever people would hear him. It is estimated that he covered 5,000 miles or more on foot in his ceaseless missionary journeys. Crowds flocked to him and were moved to tears (and to conversion) by his simple language and fiery conviction.

Powerful enemies

His enemies hated him for the success of his missions, particularly the Jansenists. This peculiar sect

January 31, 1673	—Louis-Marie Grignon de Montfort born in northwest France
1700	—Ordained a priest; shortly thereafter begins preaching career throughout France
1700-1715	—Writes Classic works *True Devotion to Mary*, *The Secret of the Rosary*, and the *Secret of Mary*
April 28, 1716	—Dies at the age of forty-three
1947	—Canonized by Pope Pius XII

emerged within the Catholic Church during the Reformation period, but some of the doctrines it held—including a flawed view of predestination and belief in total human depravity—had more in common with Calvinism than with Catholicism. And Jansenists were slippery. No sooner did the papacy condemn some of their ideas than they denied that they professed them, and pushed for reconciliation. Once they were reconciled with the Church, they would come up with more dubious ideas, generally Calvinist-leaning. Their ambiguous situation went on into the eighteenth century, and, despite further condemnations, some Jansenist attitudes seem to have survived until formally condemned by St. Pius X in the early twentieth century.

In Louis's time, the Jansenists wielded significant spiritual and political influence and they had a profound dislike for his approach to spirituality. Once Louis proposed that a large outdoor Calvary scene be erected on a hill in the countryside and hundreds of peasants worked for over a year to build it. Just before its dedication, the Jansenists succeeded on some pretext in persuading the king to order its destruction. Hundreds of peasants were now ordered to demolish their precious work, guarded by soldiers to make sure they did so. Louis must have felt the defeat keenly, but he only said, "Blessed be God! Let us build a Calvary in our hearts."

Twice Louis's powerful enemies nearly succeeded in killing him. Once they put poison in his soup; fortunately he realized it in time to take an antidote, but his health was impaired for the rest of his life. Another time, some assassins lay in wait for him, but he had a presentiment of danger and took another route. Even within the Church, he met with misunderstanding and suspicion and one bishop even

Biography

The Life of St. Louis de Montfort

placed him under interdict for a time. In Rome, however, where he went, as usual, on foot, he was given the title of Apostolic Missionary. Young people with vocations flocked to him and he founded several communities dedicated to different works: foreign missions, domestic missions, education, teaching poor children.

A Preacher and a Prophet

Still, in addition to his tireless preaching, the wonders he performed—for he had the gift of miracles—and besides the new religious orders he established, he managed, before his death, to produce several Classics of spirituality. (*True Devotion to Mary* is his best known work.) He seems also to have had the gift of prophecy, or at least to have sensed the ominous change in the spiritual and intellectual climate that the eighteenth century would bring to the world, for he wrote of a "fire in the house of God" that threatened the Church and the world with "floods of iniquity."

At length, worn out by his extraordinary labors, St. Louis de Montfort fell ill and died at only forty-three. Thousands attended the funeral of the beloved preacher. Pope Pius XII canonized him in 1947.

◆

"My Immaculate Heart shall be your refuge and the road that shall lead you to God"

—Our Lady of Fatima, 1917

"Slaves of Mary" and Other Puzzling Expressions

Followers of Montfortian spirituality in the past did not seem to find any difficulty with the terminology used in *True Devotion to Mary*. Some modern readers, however, might be uneasy with some of St. Louis's florid or seemingly antiquated expressions—especially his idea that we are to become "slaves of Mary."

What is a slave? It is a person who belongs completely to another, to be disposed of at his master's good pleasure. He always does what his master tells him to do and conforms to his wishes. We are correct in seeing the human institution of slavery as a bad thing, and in fact the Church fought against it historically. But what about being a "slave of Mary"?

As creatures made from nothing by God, we really have nothing of our own: everything we possess, from material goods to physical skills and intellectual gifts, from bodily health to supernatural virtues, comes from God. Without His keeping us in existence at every second, we would fall back into nothingness. With our total dependence on God in mind, we can see that the desire to become a slave of Mary is a great grace.

What St. Louis has us do in the Consecration to Jesus and Mary is to offer ourselves, body, soul, and everything we possess, to her to do with as she pleases. Of course she can only will what God wills, and since He always wills good for us—though we cannot always see it as such—so does she. Because we are nothing, it really is a great privilege to be allowed to make this offering to her. To become Mary's slave is to be subject to her as Our Lord Himself was during His life on earth and to do her will (which is also His) so that she can bring us closer to Him and ultimately take us to Heaven. Considering our reward, it is a one-sided bargain in our favor!

Spiritual slavery is not the only example of terminology that might seem strange, at least on first reading, to the modern reader. We are, after all, dealing with a translation from the elegant and stylized French language of the late seventeenth and early eighteenth centuries. It is the language of Racine, Moliere, Bossuet, and the great poets of the age of Louis XIV—a far cry from the plain and conversational (some would say inelegant) style of English writing we are used to.

Furthermore, the English language into which Father Faber translated the work in the nineteenth century had more in common with classical French than does today's English, but *True Devotion* has remained a popular classic in all the dozens of languages in which it now exists. St. Louis's writing style is not ours, but the beauty, strength, and value of his teaching are all timeless. ◆

The Main Apparitions of the Age of Mary

Our Lady had certainly appeared to chosen souls before the nineteenth century; one thinks, for example, of the prodigious appearances of Our Lady of Guadalupe to Juan Diego in Mexico in 1531 and the stunning "self-portrait" she left on his tilma. Starting in the early nineteenth century, however, and continuing into the twentieth, Our Lady appeared with unprecedented frequency. Here are the five most important of those apparitions, noting that many of their elements, such as requests for a greater love of and dedication to herself and her Son, are also features of St. Louis de Montfort's *True Devotion.*

To **St. Catherine Labouré**, 1830: The appearances of Our Lady to St. Catherine in her convent chapel on the Rue du Bac in Paris are among the most striking and important of Marian apparitions. They contain a definite note of prophecy, including the prediction of the overthrow of the reigning king, Charles X, which occurred during a revolution that same year, and other disasters that came to pass during the revolutions of 1848 and 1870. Our Lady's main request of St. Catherine, as a remedy for those calamities, was to have a medal struck, designed by Mary herself. She is depicted on this Miraculous Medal standing on a globe, encircled by the words, "Mary conceived without sin, pray for us who have recourse to thee." Our Lady promised abundant graces to those who would devoutly wear it.

La Salette, 1846: Our Lady's message to the children to whom she appeared was one of displeasure at the sins by which the local people were offending God, for which she warned of dire punishments including spoiled crops, famine, and death. The children were also told secrets— possibly prophecies—that have never been completely revealed. There was considerable initial skepticism on the part of Church authorities, but an extensive investigation, substantiated by miracles, led to approval of the apparition and the place became a great pilgrimage center. Large numbers of people all over France did reform their lives and the threatened chastisement was averted.

Lourdes, 1858: The series of apparitions at the southern French town of Lourdes are among the best known in history, partly due to the extraordinary outpouring of both graces and miraculous cures at the site's miraculous spring and grotto. They are also known for the response of Our Lady to Bernadette's question as to who she was: "I am the Immaculate Conception," thus divinely corroborating, as it were, the doctrine that had been defined as an article of faith by Pope Pius IX only four years previously. As in her other appearances, Mary stressed to Bernadette the need to pray for sinners, particularly in the Rosary.

Fatima, 1917: That theme of praying for sinners and making reparation for them was even more urgently stressed at Fatima. There we find all the themes of the previous apparitions recurring: the great offense to God given by the sins of men who will not reform their lives; prophecies concerning both the near future (World War I was soon to end, but another greater war would occur if Our Lady's words were not heeded) and more distant times; a secret, now revealed but still mysterious; miracles, including miraculous cures and the great Miracle of the Sun. The visions granted to the three children at Fatima resemble, in their detail and grandeur, some of the revelations described in the Bible. While some requests of Our Lady were addressed to the pope, such as the consecration of Russia, Sister Lucia emphasized that dedication to Our Lady by means of the Rosary, the prayers dictated by the Angel and by Our Lady herself, and the First Saturday devotions, were the means by which the ordinary faithful could cooperate in the salvation of the world. Again, St. Louis's devotion harmonizes with all of this. ◆

A Turbulent Time for True Devotion

King Louis XIV

The lifetime of St. Louis de Montfort, 1673-1716, encompassed an eventful period in European history for Catholics. In England, rabid anti-Catholics engineered the so-called Glorious Revolution in 1688, which involved the seizing of the throne by the Dutch Protestant William of Orange and his wife Mary (daughter of the Stuart king they were deposing), and the pursuit of determined measures to ensure that no more Catholics could ever sully the English throne.

Catholics were allowed to breathe in England, but that was about it. Meanwhile the legitimate royal family, the Stuarts, fled "over the water" to the France of St. Louis, which also welcomed hundreds of defeated Irish soldiers who chose exile rather than serve in William's army.

France Divided

In France, it was the Age of Louis XIV—a long period of French political and cultural ascendancy in Europe that included economic prosperity and a great flourishing of the arts. God had just one little favor to ask of King Louis, communicated through St. Margaret Mary Alacoque, in return for all the glory he had been given: to consecrate himself and his realm to the Sacred Heart of Jesus. Louis refused. One hundred years later, to the day, the French Revolution began.

France, although nominally Catholic, included a large Calvinist minority, known as Huguenots, who had acquired a great deal of

King Henry VIII

which held that the authority of the monarch over the Church was equal to that of the pope. Louis XIV seems to have flirted with Gallican ideas occasionally, but never went as far as the English King Henry VIII in removing his country from Catholic unity.

political and economic influence; they were officially tolerated under the Edict of Nantes, issued in 1598 in order to end the religious wars in France. But by the eighteenth century, their presence annoyed Louis XIV because they were an obstacle to religious unity. He made heavy-handed attempts to convert them, but these attempts only embittered them. Louis XIV then decided, against the prudent counsel of the pope, to revoke the Edict—which led most Hugeonots, among them scientists and other talented men that France would later miss, to emigrate; once abroad they often conspired against French national interests in any way they could.

Within the Catholic Church there were various troublesome currents such as Jansenism and Gallicanism,

The Dawn of Secularist Science

The seventeenth century was also the age of the Scientific Revolution, which transformed the intellectual life of Europe. The new scientific age saw the emergence of modern investigative methods based on experimentation, and the use of new forms of mathematics to express the findings of researchers. The unfortunate controversy over heliocentrism, precipitated by the headstrong Florentine, Galileo, would be used in these times to posit a false contradiction between science and religion that would eventually favor the growth of atheism. Among intellectuals, particularly in the eighteenth century, natural science became the measure of all things: society had to be reorganized on principles drawn from "science" rather than from religion, tradition, or pre-eighteenth-century philosophy. ◆

Strong Roots

St. Louis de Montfort's Spiritual Influences

SCRIPTURE

Luke 1:26-28
"In the sixth month the angel Gabriel was sent from God to a city of Galilee named Nazareth, to a virgin betrothed to a man whose name was Joseph, of the house of David; and the virgin's name was Mary. And he came to her and said, 'Hail, full of grace, the Lord is with you!'"

Luke 1:41-42
"And when Elizabeth heard the greeting of Mary, the babe leaped in her womb; and Elizabeth was filled with the Holy Spirit and she exclaimed with a loud cry, 'Blessed are you among women, and blessed is the fruit of your womb!'"

Luke 1:46-49
"And Mary said, 'My soul magnifies the Lord, and my spirit rejoices in God my Savior, for he has regarded the low estate of his handmaiden. For behold, henceforth all generations will call me blessed; for he who is mighty has done great things for me, and holy is his name.'"

St. Louis de Montfort's deep devotion to Mary, and his love for Jesus through her, has its origin in his spiritual formation: in the *strong roots of faith* that lie beneath the surface of every Catholic Classic. What were some of his strong roots?

Louis was such a singular personality that it is difficult to detect specific influences in his formation and teaching. He did not fit traditional categories and could be found in the most disreputable places trying to make converts. He kissed the sores of the sick, and once threw himself between two men who were trying to have a duel, seizing a sword in each hand. Bishops who invited him to preach in their dioceses often found him disconcertingly original. His response to such criticism was, "If wisdom consists in undertaking nothing new for God and in not getting oneself talked about, the apostles made a great mistake when they left Jerusalem; in any case, St. Paul should not have traveled so much so much, nor should St. Peter have set up the Cross on the Capitol."

He had been a student in a Jesuit school and certainly the *Spiritual Exercises* of St. Ignatius had some influence on the method he developed for preparing to make the consecration to Mary. When he went to the seminary in Paris, he was fortunate enough to be a student of Father Jean-Jacques Olier, the great founder of the seminary of St. Sulpice, who implemented the reform of priestly formation mandated by the Council of Trent. Olier was also very concerned about the plight of the poor (St. Vincent de Paul, who considered Oilier a saint, was one of his friends) and made a favorable impression on St. Louis. Another significant spiritual influence on St. Louis was Cardinal de Bérulle, founder of the French Oratory.

As for St. Louis's devotion to Our Lady, this was not rare during a time when the Protestant Reformation was inspiring many Catholics to defend Mary's honor—though his *True Devotion to Mary* was certainly a unique work of genius. Another special factor in St. Louis's time that greatly encouraged Marian devotion was the defense of Europe against the Turks. Louis was only ten years old when the great Battle of Vienna against the Ottoman Turks occurred, which lead the pope to call what was left of Christendom to crusade, and to implore Heaven—and the Queen of Heaven—for deliverance from the grave peril. Our Lady heard, the Turks were repulsed and driven from much of Europe, and the day of victory at Vienna became the feast day of the Most Holy Name of Mary.

"When Jesus saw his mother, and the disciple whom he loved standing near, he said to his mother, 'Woman, behold, your son!' Then he said to the disciple, 'Behold, your mother!' And from that hour the disciple took her to his own home."

—John 19:26-27

Why a Seventeenth-Century Devotion for the Twenty-First Century?

Many non-Catholics—and some Catholics, too—are given to wonder why we should give so much time and importance to devotion to Mary when our real goal is union with God? Why not go straight to Jesus? The answer, St. Louis teaches us, is that devotion to Mary is the best and surest way to Jesus, *because God wants it that way*. The Father wishes to present His Son through His mother now, just as He did 2,000 years ago.

Even those who accept this principle and wish to practice devotion to Mary might then wonder why we should turn to a book that's over 300 years old to help us do it! Wouldn't it be better to use something more up-to-date?

Of course, one might as well ask why the first-century texts of the New Testament should still apply to us. Spiritual truths are timeless, though the language in which they are expressed may change, and they are applicable to all souls in all centuries.

Devotion to Mary has been recommended by the saints of all the ages of the Church, yet it can indeed be argued that it is even more important now than in the seventeenth century, because we are living in the post-Fatima period. That most extraordinary of all Marian apparitions, with its very grave message, is a clear invitation to modern souls to entrust themselves to Mary, to practice what she taught the children to whom she appeared and to say the prayers she gave them.

Sister Lucia, one of the Fatima seers, seemed very conscious that the appearances of Our Lady were part of the final struggle between Mary and Satan, the outcome of which is foretold in Genesis (3:15). In one interview, she said she was given to understand that this struggle would be the final one.

This has led some to speculate that the end of the world is very near, though Sister Lucia never said that. It is true that saints for the past couple of centuries have spoken of "the end times" as if some kind of decisive moment in salvation history were approaching; St. Louis himself prophesied that, by means of the devotion he preached, the Church would be victorious over her enemies in some great crisis.

Surveying the condition of today's world from any point of view, there doesn't seem to be much reason for optimism about the future. Morally, the twenty-first century compares unfavorably with the late Roman period; most areas of the earth seem threatened either with war or terrorism, and even calamities of nature seem to have become more destructive.

Perhaps, indeed, there is no better time to revisit a seventeenth-century book about devotion to Mary than in our very scary and uncertain twenty-first. For whether or not we are really living in the end times, there is always help at hand in devotion to Our Lady, and aid from Jesus through her. It is surely no accident that St. Margaret Mary Alacoque, to whom devotion to the Sacred Heart was revealed, and St. Louis de Montfort, with his devotion to Our Lady, lived in the same century. The devotions to both Our Lord and to His mother go hand in hand, and total consecration to her will bring us the more surely to Him. ◆

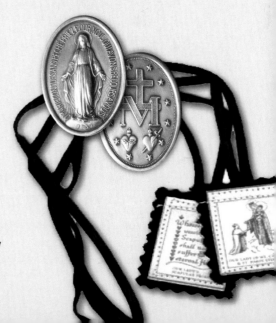

Good Fruits

The Legacy of St. Louis de Montfort

The good results produced by *True Devotion*, both in its written form and as preached by its author, are incalculable. The orders founded by St. Louis—the **Daughters of Wisdom** and the **Montfort Fathers**—have continued his work, teaching his Marian devotion through the centuries.

One of the first fruits of the saint's abundant harvest was the little known Blessed Marie Louise Trichet, later known as **Marie Louise de Jésus**. She was born in 1684 into a large, pious, upper-class family in Poitiers, France where young Father Louis had been a hospital chaplain.

One day when she was seventeen, Marie Louise went to confession to the saint and told him of her desire for a religious vocation. Under Father Louis's direction, her discernment was to take an odd form, not especially pleasing to her family ("You will become as mad as that priest!" said her mother). Marie Louise was told first to help the poor patients in that badly run hospital, but when she volunteered, there was no position for her, so she took the unusual step of entering the institution as an inmate. Once inside, she gradually brought about improvements and, having consecrated herself to the religious life in receiving the habit from St. Louis as the first of the Daughters of Wisdom, she was eventually made the administrator of the hospital. The remaining four decades of her life were spent in nursing the sick, serving the poor, and teaching children.

Father Frederick Faber, the great spiritual writer, convert, and collaborator of John Henry Newman in founding Oratories to evangelize England, discovered the work of St. Louis de Montfort in the mid-nineteenth century and produced the first English translation of *True Devotion*. From his own fifteen years' experience of studying and practicing what St. Louis preached, he wrote, "those who take him for their master will hardly be able to name a saint or ascetical writer to whose grace and spirit their mind will be more subject than to his . . . I cannot think of a higher work or a broader vocation for anyone than the simple spreading of this . . . devotion."

In the early twentieth century, **Pope St. Pius X** wrote, "I heartily recommend *True Devotion to the Blessed Virgin*, so admirably written by Blessed de Montfort [this was before his canonization], and to all who read it grant the Apostolic

Benediction." **Pope Pius XI** said that he had "practiced the devotion ever since my youth," while **Pope Leo XIII** had granted a plenary indulgence to those who made St. Louis de Montfort's Act of Consecration to the Blessed Virgin. He renewed his own act on his deathbed, invoking the aid of St. Louis.

Sister Lucia of Fatima, in speaking with a Montfort priest in 1946, indicated that she knew of St. Louis and his doctrine, though she had not read his books, and that she loved and practiced the devotion.

Finally, the **Legion of Mary**, founded by Frank Duff in 1921, is perhaps the most visible fruit of the teachings of St. Louis de Montfort in our time. With tens of thousands of members throughout and a spirituality based on True Devotion, it continues to spread the teaching and spirit of the saint in daily life.

> **DID YOU KNOW?**
> *St. Louis de Montfort prophesied that those who are specially devoted to Mary will be instrumental in defeating the Antichrist.*

"Mary adorns her clients with her merits, assists them with her power, enlightens them with her light, and kindles them with her love. She imparts her virtues to them and becomes their security, their intercessor, and their all with Jesus."

—St. Louis de Montfort

How to Read *True Devotion to Mary*

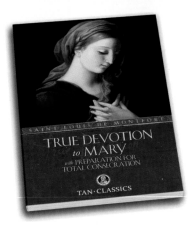

A Catholic Classic is not like other books. Properly read and meditated upon, it nourishes not only the mind but the soul: effecting in the reader an increase in holiness as well as knowledge. Follow this guide, based on the advice of St. Alphonsus Liguori, to get the maximum benefit from *True Devotion to Mary*.

First, set aside a quiet place and time. Novels and newspapers can be read on the bus or in a noisy house, but not a Catholic Classic. Pray before you begin, asking God to teach you the lessons he wants you to learn. Ask for St. Louis de Montfort to be present, praying for and with you.

Have the right intentions. The purpose of spiritual reading is to grow in love of God and divine things, not to acquire facts, learn arguments, or indulge superficial curiosity. We shouldn't read a Classic just to say we have read it; we should read it because we want to be changed by it.

Read slowly and with attention. Like food that must be chewed carefully, spiritual reading requires some work in order to draw out its nutrients. Don't be afraid to linger over passages, prayerfully re-reading sections that confuse you or make a strong impression on you. Let's be like bees, says St. Alphonsus, who "do not pass from one flower to another until they have gathered all the nectar they found in the first."

Finally, take what you've learned and put it into practice. Form a concrete intention to do this as you approach and as you finish each session of reading. Having received the spiritual wisdom of the saints, carry it with you in your heart, and put it to work in service of God and neighbor.

Consecration Prayer of St. Louis de Montfort

I, [name], a faithless sinner, renew and ratify today in thy hands, O Immaculate Mother, the vows of my Baptism. I renounce forever Satan, his pomps and works, and I give myself entirely to Jesus Christ, the Incarnate Wisdom, to carry my cross after Him all the days of my life, and to be more faithful to Him than I have ever been before.

In the presence of all the heavenly court I choose thee, this day for my Mother and Mistress. I deliver and consecrate to thee, as thy slave, my body and soul, my goods, both interior and exterior, and even the value of all my good actions, past, present and future, leaving to thee the entire and full right of disposing of me, and all that belongs to me, without exception, according to thy good pleasure, for the greater glory of God, in time and in eternity. Amen.

Putting It into Practice

Once you have finished reading and meditating on *True Devotion*, you might set aside a few days to try putting it into practice. The final section of the book provides suggestions for preparing to make the consecration to Jesus through Mary. St. Louis proposes a twelve-day period of preparation, plus three weeks devoted to knowledge of self, knowledge of the Blessed Virgin, and knowledge of Jesus Christ. If we were to adjust those proposals to fit a one-week period, it might look like this:

Day 1: Examine Your Attachments

St. Louis writes, "The first part of the preparation should be employed in casting off the spirit of the world, which is contrary to that of Jesus Christ." He goes on to refer to the manifestations of this spirit of the world in the concupiscence of the flesh, concupiscence of the eyes, and the pride of life. Spend the first day in examining your life for little gratifications and self-indulgences that you might give up for a week

as a sacrifice. There are often very small, harmless things to which we have become attached that really do cost us something to give up for a time: that cookie after lunch or the breakfast donut. The point is to use your prayer time on this day to look for attachments to physical gratifications that might interfere with your total dedication to Christ and to Mary.

Day 2: Practice Custody of the Eyes

Today, pay attention to what your eyes are doing even while you are not consciously focusing them. The desire to acquire the things of this world is aroused by our view of them: nice clothes, jewelry, cars. Resolve to practice serious custody of the eyes throughout this week (no idle window-shopping or online browsing!).

Day 3: Watch for Pride

The pride of life has been interpreted in various ways, but it always involves seeing ourselves as the source of whatever gifts we have

True Devotion to Mary

or the good that we do. We can be proud of our looks, skills, well-behaved children, college degrees, or anything else that enhances us in the eyes of others—or that we think does so. Today, examine your life for manifestations of pride and pray for the grace of true self-knowledge and humility. Practice some small mortification related to the virtue of humility every day this week.

Day 4: Know Yourself

Today we should pray for true knowledge of ourselves, the sins we have committed throughout our lives, and how much we need God's help to overcome our misery. This will help us to enter seriously on the efficacious but easy way of devotion to Mary.

Day 5: Study Mary

Today we will try to come to know Mary better. We can do this by reading the sections of the Gospels included by St. Louis in his "preparation" section, meditating on the differ-

ent virtues Our Lady practiced, and praying to her for help in imitating her as much as we can.

Day 6: Study Jesus

This day should be devoted to the knowledge of Jesus Christ. We should first follow the reading suggestions of St. Louis, and then meditate prayerfully on what we have read. We will consider His relationship with His Blessed Mother throughout His life and pray for her help in imitating Him.

Day 7: Look Back and Pray for Grace

Today, we can look back over the work of the past week and review what we have done on each day. If we feel ready to make the act of consecration, we can do it today; if not, this is the day to pray for the grace to become ready. We should also thank God and Our Lady for the graces we have undoubtedly received this week.

"Through Mary, the miserable obtain mercy, the graceless find grace, and sinners receive pardon."

—St. Augustine of Hippo (354–430)

Words to Know

Age of Mary: The period from the early nineteenth to the early twentieth century in which five major Marian apparitions occurred. The frequency and urgency of these messages is unprecedented and unequaled.

Consecration: A special act of honor and veneration, for the purpose of making something or someone holy.

Huguenots: The French Calvinist minority during the sixteenth and seventeenth centuries. Most left France with the revocation of the Edict of Nantes, which had previously guaranteed religious tolerance.

Hyperdulia: Latin term for the kind of devotion due to Mary: less than the *latria* (divine worship) due to God, but greater than the *dulia* (reverence) we give the saints.

Gallicanism: Heresy that flourished in the seventeenth century, declaring that the civil government has equal or greater authority over the local Church than the pope does.

Jansenism: Another seventeenth century heresy that adopted Calvinist ideas about salvation. Jansenists denied human free will and were sometimes known for their severe moral practices.

Legion of Mary: A Catholic lay movement that evangelizes and practices works of mercy around the world. The Legion's spiritual principles are taken in great part from de Montfort's writings.

Mediatrix: A title given to Mary, expressing the Catholic teaching that God gives grace to the world through her, just as He gave Jesus to the world through her.

Protestant Reformation: The doctrinal and ecclesial revolution that in the sixteenth and seventeenth centuries saw many parts of Catholic Europe—particularly England, Scandinavia, and parts of Germany—break from the Church into various national churches, denominations, and sects.

Rosary: A popular Marian devotion that involves vocal prayer coupled with meditation on the mysteries of Christ's life, using a string of beads to keep track of the prayers said.

Additional Resources & Suggested Reading

For those who enjoyed *True Devotion to Mary*, there are more works by St. Louis, all of them brief, sometimes only pamphlet-size, but full of his extraordinary wisdom combined with practicality.

A work by another saint, who, like St. Louis was born in the seventeenth century and died in the eighteenth, is *The Glories of Mary* by St. Alphonsus Liguori, (TAN Books, 1977). This is a compendium of information on Mary, along with suggestions for developing devotion to her, all done in a simple and lively style illustrated with numerous anecdotes.

The Love of Eternal Wisdom (Montfort Publications, 1960) is closely related to *True Devotion* and helps the reader make the connection between the imitation of Christ and devotion to Mary. The final chapter introduces the concepts developed in *True Devotion*, clarifying some of the points made there.

The Secret of Mary (TAN Books, 1998) is a small book, appealingly written, in which St. Louis clarifies some of the points (such as his use of the word "slave") that he made in *True Devotion*. It is a little gem of spirituality.

In the popular *Secret of the Rosary* (TAN Books, 1976), St. Louis analyzes the many facets of this great means of praying to and meditating upon Our Lady and Christ. He was so convinced of the efficacy of the Rosary as a means of salvation that he obtained permission to found Rosary Confraternities, which spread and flourished throughout a large part of France in his lifetime.